WRITING VIVID CHARACTERS

D1731294

by Rayne Hall

WRITING VIVID CHARACTERS

Book cover by Erica Syverson

© 2016 Rayne Hall

July 2016 Edition

ISBN-13: 978-1535136327 ISBN-10: 1535136324

CONTENTS

INTRODUCTION

Do you want to create compelling characters about whom the readers care deeply?

This book reveals professional techniques to invent individuals who are so real that your readers will love or hate, fear or root for them, and so fascinating that your readers will remember them forever.

This is not a beginner's guide. I assume that you have mastered the basics of fiction writing, and don't need an explanation of what characterisation is and why it matters for your story. But your characters may not be as memorable as your story deserves. Perhaps they are too similar to one another, perhaps they don't jump off the page like real people, and perhaps they lack that certain something that makes them unforgettable.

I'll offer you a toolbox filled with techniques. These are not 'rules' every writer must follow, but suggestions you can adapt to suit your vision. You can use this guide to create a cast of characters from scratch, or you can power up the characters about whom you've written a draft.

As an experienced writer, you're probably familiar with some of the techniques I discuss. Use those sections as a refresher course and for a fresh perspective on what you already know.

If you're a novice at fiction writing, I suggest you put this book aside for now and start with a beginner-level guide.

To illustrate my points, I'll give examples from one of my books, the dark epic fantasy novel *Storm Dancer.* You don't need to read the book to understand the examples.

When referring to readers and characters, I'll sometimes use 'she' and sometimes 'he', simply to avoid the clunky 'he or she' constructions. If you're used to American English, my British word choices, syntax, grammar, punctuation and spelling may look unfamiliar, but you shouldn't have any difficulty understanding them.

Now let's have fun bringing the cast of your book to life.

Rayne Hall

CHAPTER 1:
RECRUITING YOUR CAST

You're the CEO of your book and in charge of whom you hire. When recruiting characters for a new project, you may have clear specifications for some roles, but only vague ideas for others. Occasionally, characters simply walk into the plot uninvited and behave as if they belong.

FROM CHARACTER TO PLOT, FROM PLOT TO CHARACTER

Developing characters in depth is a good idea. You need to know them as well as the members of your family or your closest friends, and this book is going to help you. The question is, when should you create this character profile – before you start writing, or as you go along?

A related question is what comes first, character or plot? I believe that characters shape the plot, and the plot shapes the characters. It's best to develop them organically, side by side. Creating first one and then the other can lead to inauthentic stories.

If you start by creating a character with a full history, strengths, weaknesses, ambitions, traits, hopes and fears, and then write a story about him, you may discover that he isn't at all who he seemed to be. As he comes alive, he'll reject the profile you prescribed for him. His reactions to plot events reveal what kind of person he really is.

If you begin with a plot, and then recruit a character to act it out, you may find that he'll refuse to behave the way you intended. He'll do what he wants to do, especially if he's the strong-willed type, leaving you with no choice but to change the plot.

I'm in favour of allowing characters to develop gradually and getting to know them as the plot unfolds. However, it helps to have a broad idea of each character, at least the important ones, before you start writing about them.

For instance, you probably know the gender and age group.

For the main character, I suggest you specify a trait which will encourage him to get into trouble – 'curious' or 'courageous' are useful.

The kind of book you're writing also gives clues about characters. For example, the main character in a thriller is tenacious, determined, with a strong sense of justice, probably with a law enforcement background and fighting skills. In a traditional romance, the 'love interest' character is male, handsome, confident, considerate, powerful and single.

PUT OUT A CASTING CALL

To recruit characters for your novel, compile a job advertisement or a casting call. Although you can do this mentally, I suggest putting it in writing.

"Wanted:

Female Lead for YA Novel.

Age 14-17, student, single. Must be curious, musical and active in sports.

Job involves some travel and music performances.

Pets and personal insecurities welcome."

"Wanted:

Private Investigator.

Male, 18+. Courageous, tenacious, quick-thinking, resourceful, loyal.

Must have law enforcement background, preferably in homicide or vice.

Single father (widowed or divorced) preferred.

Tough youth (poverty, slum-dwelling, parental neglect), under-world connections and martial arts skills an advantage

Job involves some fighting and considerable discomfort and danger."

"Serial Killer Required

male, white, 22-29. Must be esteemed community member, hand-some and popular.

IQ 130 higher. Needs excellent people skills

No previous criminal record, but experience in animal torture and minor arson desirable."

Unlike real-life job advertisements, these posts don't need to be po-litically correct. You can specify age, gender, ethnicity, even sexual orientation.

Once you've formulated the casting call, relax and allow applicants to pop into your head. They will come before long, probably within a day or so when you sit down with a paper and a notebook.

If you post the advertisements immediately before going to bed, your subconscious will search them out overnight and you may wake knowing exactly who they are.

INTERVIEWING THE CANDIDATES

Don't hire them without an interview, and don't believe everything they claim. In their eagerness to get the job, some characters tell lies, so ask probing questions.

I suggest you do the following exercise, which is a lot of fun … but do it in private, not in your local coffee shop.

Get out two chairs. Sit on the first one. In the role of recruiter/human resources officer/casting director, ask questions, such as:

"You witness a mugging – two attackers against a lone woman. They have knives, you are unarmed. What do you do?"

"Your boyfriend breaks up with you by text message to take up with a more glamorous girl. How do you react?"

"This job involves hiding in a stinking rubbish skip for three hours. How do you feel about that?"

Ask the questions out loud, one at a time. After each question, switch to the other chair. Now you're the job applicant. Answer the question out loud.

This method leads to astonishing insights into the character, not just in what he says, but in how he says it. Does he hesitate, evade, or answer with confidence? Does he enjoy the interview, or do certain questions make him squirm?

Even with an in-depth interview, characters won't tell you the truth about everything, and you'll learn their secrets only later. That's OK – as long as the character is right for the job, unexpected facets of their personality and situations will enrich the plot.

Some characters won't audition for a role, but wait until the story is underway, then simply walk onto the set and interact with the other actors. It's up to you what to do with them. Either chase them away – be firm! – or give them a small part if their presence enriches the book.

FROM MY PERSONAL EXPERIENCE

When I wrote my dark-epic fantasy novel *Storm Dancer*, I recruited some characters after careful planning, but also hired others who simply turned up. Despite thorough interviews and ability checks, I got some big surprises later.

Expecting to write a standard adventure quest fantasy, I advertised for a hero with courage and sword-fighting skills. **Dahoud** presented himself as lively swashbuckling type. He said he was working as a clerk and keen go on an adventure. He mentioned briefly that he had served in the army for a while, but didn't go into detail. It didn't occur to me to ask for how long and in what capacity.

I had written 70,000 words of draft before I discovered that Dahoud was possessed by a demon! That changed everything. I had to rewrite the whole book with a new plot. The intended storyline became a mere background to the real story. *Storm Dancer* took on a decidedly dark slant.

Far from being the happy extroverted swashbuckler he had acted during the interview, Dahoud turned out to be a dark, brooding character with a dangerous secret.

And the demon wasn't his only secret, as I discovered when I had nearly completed the second draft. Dahoud finally told me that he wasn't who he seemed. His stint in the army, which I had taken to mean a few months, had been a long career culminating in him being the nation's most celebrated general. To start a new life, he had faked his own death and funeral.

Even that was not all. After another rewrite, he admitted that when he was a general, he had brutally devastated a region... and it was the region where I had sent him as a peaceful benign ruler. The general's brutality was still remembered, and mothers used his name to scare children into obedience. He confessed that if the natives discovered who he really was, they would tear him to shreds, so he had to make sure nobody ever found out.

The belated discoveries forced repeated rewrites, but they also enriched the story. The demon gave the book psychological depth of a struggle between good and evil within one person. The secret identity built wonderful tension. Near the end of the novel, I revealed who Dahoud really was – or rather, I forced him to reveal it himself.

For the role of Dahoud's best friend, I advertised for someone loyal, diplomatic and cultured, with political ambitions. **Tarkan** genuinely met all those criteria. What he didn't tell me during the interview is that he was gay. Since he was acting straight, I didn't have an inkling until the second draft. Eventually, I realised that Tarkan's orientation added value to the plot. In a fiercely homophobic society, where being outed meant execution, a likeable gay character created a balance and made the readers care. On top of that, the close friendship between Tarkan and Dahoud (who for a long time did not know) incited useful conflicts.

For the role of **Merida,** I wanted someone with pluck, courage, education, honesty and strong principles. Strong principles she had – but I realised only belatedly how prudish and patronising she could be! Of course I had fun putting her in situations which challenged her principles, and watching her squirm. Her unbending attitude, and being forced to adapt, led to entertaining plot situations.

Since she learnt tolerance and gradually grew to be more open-minded, readers come to like her a lot, even if they dislike her at first.

When I appointed **Kirral** as ruler of the country, I saw that he was highly intelligent and a shrewd observer of human nature, which was what I wanted. I neglected to carry out a background check. Big mistake! Kirral turned out to be a sadist who used his power to find victims to torment. Of course this meant altering the plot to make Kirral the villain. This led to interesting plot complications, especially when he chose as his next victim the plucky Merida. Kirral gets more fan mail than any of my other characters. Readers love him – from a distance.

Yora didn't apply for a job. She simply walked into the plot. Dahoud had to prove his mettle by competing against the region's most ferocious fighters, one after the other. He had just won one match and lost another, and was waiting for his next opponent. I was as surprised as Dahoud when this spunky thirteen-year-old girl came running into the arena. She was so good that I allowed her to stay and play an important part in several scenes.

ASSIGNMENT

Create job advertisements for three characters. Specify what background, experience and skills they must have, and what is desirable but not essential.

CHAPTER 2:
WHAT TYPES OF CHARACTERS DO YOU NEED?

Let's start with the most important member of the team: the main character (MC for short).

GET TO KNOW YOUR MAIN CHARACTER

The main character is the central figure in your plot, the person around whom the story revolves. Spend time getting to know this person: you need to know him as well as you know a member of your family or your closest friend.

Every novel has a main character. Some novels have more than one. For example, if a novel spans several generations, it may be told in several parts, each section following a character from the current generation.

The technical term for the main character is 'protagonist'. In Fantasy and Adventure fiction, he is often also called the 'hero' – and this can get confusing, because in the Romance genre, the term 'hero' refers not to the main character, but to her male love interest. Let's stick to 'MC' so you'll know which character I'm talking about.

POINT OF VIEW

When you tell the story from the perspective of a character, this is called Point of View. Get deep inside this character's head and heart, because the reader will share his experience. Show only what the PoV character sees, hears, smells, thinks and feels. The deeper you delve into the PoV, the more intensely the reader will experience the story.

Anything the PoV doesn't experience, the reader won't experience either, so choose a PoV character who is present at all crucial story events.

If you use Point of View in your novel, then the MC is probably (but not necessarily) the PoV character.

If you want to find out more about PoV, you may want to look at my guide *Writing Deep Point of View.* It works well as a continuation of this book.

DEVELOP THE CHARACTER FROM THE INSIDE OUT

While it's useful to take note of your MC's tastes and habits, postpone choosing his breakfast habits and his clothing style until you know him better.

Start the characterisation with what's deep inside – values, hopes, fears and such – and only then move on to hobbies, favourite foods, mannerisms and fashion sense.

If you decide the outward stuff before the core, it will feel forced. It's much better to start at the core and develop the rest from there.

If you enjoy working with character questionnaires, you'll find many on the web. Choose one which starts with the inner values and gradually moves outwards, or rearrange the order of the questions before you answer them.

HOW MANY CHARACTERS DOES YOUR NOVEL NEED?

The longer the novel, the more characters you can and should involve. Four is the minimum, but a long novel can easily have forty or more.

Introduce no more than two new characters at a time. Otherwise your readers will get confused and forget their names and who they are.

MAJOR CHARACTERS

Characters who play an important role in the plot are called 'major characters'. They appear in many scenes, and their actions change the plot.

Most novels have an antagonist – a character who works against the MC. This is often a rival, opponent or enemy. Long novels may have more than one antagonist. If the antagonist is evil, he's also called a 'villain'. Spend time developing the antagonist, and make him a worthy foe for your MC. The antagonist should be intelligent, resourceful and brave. The greater the antagonist is, the greater the MC becomes. Don't make him all bad, even if he's a villain, but give him at least one genuine redeeming trait.

The 'love interest' is the person whom the MC is romantically drawn to or involved with, and often commits to at the end of the book. In Romance, the love interest is the most important character after the MC.

Spend time developing the major characters, again creating them from the inside out. A typical novel has between three and twenty major characters, not counting the MC, but this is not a rule.

To give your novel complexity without making it over-long, use each major character in several ways. The MC's ballet teacher could also be the love interest's sister, and the nosy neighbour could be the home-care nurse who looks after the MC's dying mum.

MINOR CHARACTERS

Named characters with individual personalities who have speaking parts are called 'minor' characters. They may appear in several scenes, though not necessarily in all parts of the book. Their actions affect what happens in that scene, but not the long-term outcome. You could delete a minor character from the book, and the story would still play out in much the same way.

While you don't need to develop the minor characters in great depth, they have to be individuals. Minor characters are a great way to introduce humour and light relief into your plot. Make them as quirky as the people you know in real life. Show their clothing style, speech patterns and mannerisms to entertain your readers.

SPEAR-CARRIERS

This term comes from the world of theatre, where scripts sometimes call for 'two men carrying spears'. They are of no importance to the plot. Even if they appear in more than one scene, they could be replaced by others. Although human, they fulfil the same function as a prop or piece of furniture, except they can move. They don't have lines to speak, and don't have individual personalities so there's no need to develop them as fully fleshed-out characters.

Here's an example of spear-carriers in fiction:

Two priestesses led the procession, followed by the government ministers, the highest-ranking nobles of the realm, and finally, on a magnificent black horse, the Queen herself. Resplendent in a bejewelled dress, she....

In this case, the priestesses, ministers and nobles are all spear-carriers.

To help the reader see the scene, you may want to give a clue about what the spear-carriers look like:

Two gaunt men

An old woman

A plump toddler

A gaggle of teenage girls in too-short skirts

But don't describe the spear-carrier in detail, or your readers will expect him to play a role in the plot.

FROM MY PERSONAL EXPERIENCE

Storm Dancer is my longest novel at 160K words, and the cast is large.

Besides the MC Dahoud, major characters are Merida, the djinn (Dahoud's demonic antagonist), Kirral (the human antagonist), Esha, Yora, Tarkan, Teruma, Haurvatat, Khadiffe, Paniour, Mansour (antagonist at the beginning of the book, but his role changes later), Baryush (antagonist in the later part of the book), Govan, Naima, Keera, Wurran, Sirria, Yann, the whiteseer, Zun. That's twenty major characters in addition to the MC.

I haven't counted the minor ones – there are lots, from the belly dance teacher in the harem to the snobbish palace guard, from the gossipy matron to the lecherous landlord of the Black Dog Inn.

ASSIGNMENT

Draw up a tentative list of major characters. See if you can merge any.

Think of a minor character who could enliven a scene. A surly waitress, an overeager museum guide? Give him quirks to entertain the reader.

CHAPTER 3:
WHAT DOES THE MC WANT?

While you can leave most character features to decide as you go along, I recommend you define the MC's core goal at the start, because it will drive the plot.

CHOOSE THE GOAL

The MC's main goal should be something the character really, really wants – perhaps even needs – and it must not be easy to achieve.

The goal can and should drive most of the character's actions. At the end of the book, the MC and the reader know whether she has achieved it.

Here are some goal examples:

- To find out who her biological father really is
- To gain a sports scholarship for college
- To catch the serial killer before he strikes again
- To defeat the monster and save the kingdom
- To win the elixir and bring it home

MOTIVATION

Next, choose the motivation, the reason why the character wants this goal so desperately. Actually, I recommend giving her more than one good reason. Aim for at least three, and more is better.

These reasons can be public or personal, official or secret, big or small, idealistic or materialistic, selfish or selfless. Mix them up.

Let's say the MC's goal is to find out who her biological father really is. Why does she want to discover this information?

- She yearns for a clear sense of self and identity
- She needs to be sure that the man she's in love with is not her half-brother
- She wants to defy her domineering mother just once – and the mother forbade her to investigate
- She wants to know what her ethnic heritage is
- An aspiring private investigator, she wants to practice her detecting skills
- She wants to satisfy her curiosity

WHAT'S AT STAKE?

Why is this so important to her? Go through her reasons one by one, and think of the terrible consequences if she fails.

Examples:

If she doesn't find out who her biological father is, she may get wed and forever wonder if she's married her own half-brother.

If she doesn't defy her mother in this, she'll never summon the courage to stand up to her dictatorial ways in other matters.

THE UNACKNOWLEDGED NEED

Besides the character's declared goal, there may be another need, something she won't admit to herself, let alone to others. This is a deep, psychological need, and the character can't be truly happy until it is met. In Romance fiction, this is often the need to be loved.

The unacknowledged need can be independent from the stated goal, or related to it. For example, if the MC's stated goal is to find who her biological father is, then her unacknowledged need may be to reconcile with her mother. The unacknowledged need can even be at odds with the stated goal.

To satisfy your readers, make sure that this secret need is both acknowledged and fulfilled at the end of the book, even if the stated goal is lost.

GOALS FOR OTHER CHARACTERS

Consider giving every character in your novel a goal, not just the MC, though you don't need to develop them in as much depth as the MC's. The antagonist and the love interest should definitely have goals.

FROM MY PERSONAL EXPERIENCE

In *Storm Dancer*, **Dahoud's** big goal is to defeat his demon, and his unacknowledged inner need is to find a woman's love.

Merida's goal is to gain more value points to elevate her status in society. Her unacknowledged need is almost the opposite: deep down she yearns to be appreciated for something other than her value points and social status.

With both characters, I discovered the unacknowledged need only after I got to know them really well.

ASSIGNMENT

What is your MC's big goal, the one that drives the novel plot?

Think of at least five reasons why she wants or needs this.

What is her inner need, the unacknowledged yearning that drives her although she doesn't know it yet?

CHAPTER 4:
SHOW DON'T TELL TRAITS

Try not to tell your readers what a character is like. Show it.

HOW TO CONVEY CHARACTERISTICS

Find little ways to weave behaviourisms into the story. The reader will observe these clues – consciously or subconsciously, and conclude that this is the character's personality.

Example: Fastidious Character

Let's say Mary, a major character, is a fastidious person who is particular about cleanliness and tidiness.

Instead of writing 'Mary was fastidious', show her behaving in fastidious ways. When entering a friend's home, she wipes her shoes thoroughly on the doormat. At the entrance to her own house, a boot-scraper and two doormats greet the visitor, together with a sign: 'wipe your shoes, please'. While waiting, she flicks bits of fluff from her clothes. When local authorities propose stringent street-cleaning measures, she approves enthusiastically. She cleans up after her flatmate rather than leaving the place dirty, and tidies things away even if others have only just left them.

Example: Stingy Character

Is Mary a stingy person? Show her performing many small actions of thrift, including some which are decidedly ungenerous.

She measures the milk carefully before serving coffee, estimating how much will be needed for the number of people. As soon as everyone has had one biscuit, she removes the tin from the table.

When she invites guests for dinner, she serves everyone a precise portion rather than let them help themselves.

She clips coupons and buys groceries on special offer, walking from shop to shop to get the best bargain rather than buying everything in one place and paying the full price.

She admonishes her kids to open the Christmas gifts carefully. Then she smooths and folds the wrapping paper and saves it in the box for use next year, together with any ribbons and reusable greetings cards.

After phoning friends, she ends the conversation, asking them to ring her back.

Example: Caring Character

If Mary is a caring person, don't tell the reader 'Mary was the caring type'. Instead, show several times how she offers to help someone without being asked. When the MC has suffered an injury or upset, Mary phones the next day to find out how he is and if he needs support. When meeting a customer or a neighbour, Mary enquires after his children's progress and his wife's health.

Example: Vain Character

If Mary is vain, show her catching glimpses of herself in reflective surfaces such as windows. The walls of Mary's home feature mirrors and photos of Mary herself. She frequently pats her hair.

Example: Reliable Character

If Mary is reliable, show her checking her diary, watch and schedule to make sure she does what she committed to. She cuts short an interesting visit in order to be punctual for an appointment, turns down a lucrative deal rather than let down an existing customer, and goes out of her way to keep a promise even when it's a huge inconvenience.

CHOOSING AND USING CHARACTER TRAITS

Decide on several traits for each character. If possible, condense them into adjectives (sarcastic, fun-loving, ambitious, musical, brooding, aggressive, devious, clever, loyal, honourable, chaste etc.)

How many traits should each character have? I suggest two for minor characters, four or five for major characters, five or six for the main character.

Of course your characters are more complex than four to six words. But by selecting the most important characteristics, you can get to the essence. If you use too many, this essence gets diluted. On the other hand, if you use too few characteristics, the characters will feel flat.

For minor characters, pick quirky habits to convey their traits. This can add entertainment and humour to your story, even when the main plot is grim.

COMPILING IDEAS

Write each characteristic at the top of a page. Beneath, write ideas how this trait might show in action. This file may take days or weeks to compile. Add to it as you observe real life people, research on the internet, and brainstorm with friends.

Keep all the files you've compiled, because you may want to expand them later and adapt them for other characters in future works.

Here's an optional project for serious fiction writers: create a collection of character traits. Observe people around you – the way they behave at the supermarket checkout or in the coffee shop. What trait does this behaviour indicate? Write it in your notebook.

Do you know someone who often says 'I'd love to, but...' and who always agrees with the person she's talking to, even though she's expressed the opposite opinion to someone else? This could mean she's a hypocrite. Write these behaviours in your notebook under 'hypocritical'.

Do you have a shy friend who answers only 'yes' or 'no' to questions and often veils her face with her hand? Record those behaviours under the heading 'shy'.

Before long, you'll have compiled a whole thesaurus of character traits and behaviours you can draw on for future works of fiction.

FROM MY PERSONAL EXPERIENCE

Although I find it useful to list key traits of important characters before I start writing, in practice they always change during the process.

As I write, I observe the characters' behaviours. I identify the underlying character trait, and then find more behaviourisms to reflect it.

Dahoud, the MC of *Storm Dancer,* is nothing like how I pictured him at the beginning. He's still courageous and honourable – but not spontaneous, adventurous, witty and sarcastic. Instead I found him to be serious, assertive, responsible and compassionate.

Merida is as honest and principled as I thought she would be – but instead of musical and romantic she's resourceful and patronising.

Of all characters, only **Tarkan** remained largely as I saw him first: intelligent, diplomatic, cultured, loyal and ambitious.

ASSIGNMENT

Choose one character to work with – perhaps the MC.

Make a list of the character's core attributes. If you have too many ideas, try to narrow them down. If you can express them in adjectives, that's best. (This list is not set in stone. As you write and get to know the character better, you may choose to cross out some and add others.)

Then think of ways how these could be expressed. Remember people you've known in real life who had those traits, and how their behaviour revealed those characteristics. For each character trait, think of at least three ways to show it. More is better. Can you think of ten or twenty?

Later, whenever you write a scene featuring this character, try to weave at least one of those behaviourisms into the action.

CHAPTER 5:
HOW TO MAKE YOUR MAIN CHARACTER LIKEABLE

Make the readers like the MC from the first page, so they look forward to spending many hours in his company.

Here are two techniques you can use.

1. Make the MC an 'Underdog'

Readers root for characters who are at a disadvantage. Find a way to present your MC as lesser-privileged – but not cowed by it – and readers will sympathise.

Could she be wheelchair-bound, limping or blind, and thus unable to join certain activities? Maybe his face is scarred by pockmarks, or so disfigured by burns that his ugliness scares people. She might belong to an ethnic minority and can't get a good job, or come from a family of good-for-nothings and therefore get the blame for every neighbourhood crime. His classmates may mock him because of his stutter, or look down on him because he wears hand-me-downs while they show off their designer clothes.

Even if your character comes from a privileged background, you can find an 'underdog' angle: what if he's the king's youngest son and therefore of no importance? Perhaps being a girl in a patriarchal society means she can't get the education she yearns for. Or what if the boy gets neglected in favour of his mother's children from her new marriage?

Use your creativity to come up with an 'underdog' angle, and establish it in the opening scene, ideally on the first page.

What not to do:

Don't let the MC whine about his fate, or even comment or dwell on it. That would lessen the reader's admiration. Instead, he ignores the taunts and makes the best of the bad situation.

2. Make the MC help someone less fortunate than himself

Establish the MC as a likeable person by showing how she does a small act of kindness in the first scene. Ideally, she is helping someone who is helpless.

Perhaps she sees a trapped puppy and frees it. Maybe he tells the men who verbally harass a woman to stop. She may witness a classmate getting bullied and step in. Even a simple act such as holding the door open for a wheelchair user or a pram-pushing mum serves.

This method is super-effective when combined with the 'underdog' effect. Readers admire a character who, while suffering himself, still helps those who are suffering more. What if her wealthy fellow students snub her because she can't afford to join them in the cafeteria, and then she gives her modest lunch money to a hungry homeless person?

To increase the impact, show that nobody else is making an effort. Perhaps everyone pushes past the frail old man struggling to climb the stairs. Or perhaps people want to help, but lack the courage and resourcefulness. A whole crowd may have gathered, staring up at the balcony where a toddler is stuck in the railing, terrified of what will happen if the kid falls – and your MC climbs up and gets him free.

What not to do:

Don't dwell on the good deed. The MC doesn't make a big deal out of it, and neither should you. Let the MC act in a casual way, as a matter of course without dwelling on it, and immediately move on to what he has set out to do.

Example

Here's an example from one of my own books, *Storm Dancer,* where I combined these two techniques to gain sympathy for Dahoud:

Even in the shade of the graffiti-carved olive tree, the air sang with heat. Dahoud listened to the hum of voices in the tavern garden, the murmured gossip about royals and rebels. If patrons noticed him, they would only see a young clerk sitting among the lord-satrap's followers, a harmless bureaucrat. Dahoud planned to stay harmless.

The tavern bustled with women – whiteseers hanging about in the hope of earning a copper, traders celebrating deals, belly dancers clinking finger cymbals – women who neither backed away from him nor screamed.

The youngest of the entertainers wound her way between the benches towards their table, the tassels on her slender hips bouncing, the rows of copper rings on her sash tinkling with every snaky twist. Since she seemed nervous, as if it was her first show, he sent her an encouraging smile. Ignoring him, she shimmied to Lord Govan.

The djinn slithered inside Dahoud, stirring a stream of fury, whipping his blood into a hot storm. Would she dare to disregard the Black Besieger? What lesson would he teach to punish her insolence?

Dahoud stared past her sweat-glistening torso, the urge to subdue her washing over him in a boiling wave. For three years, he had battled against the djinn's temptations. To indulge in fantasies would batter his defences and breach his resistance. He focused on the flavours on his tongue, the tart citron juice and the sage-spiced mutton, on the tender texture of the meat.

Govan clasped the dancer's wrist and drew her close. "Come, honey-flower, let's see your blossoms."

She tried to pull herself from his grip. Panic painted her face. Against a lesser man's groping, she might defend herself with slaps and screams, but this was the lord-satrap. She was too young to know how to slip out of such a situation, and none of her older colleagues on the far side of the garden noticed her plight. The other clerks at the table laughed.

"My Lord," Dahoud said. "She doesn't want your attentions."

"She's only a belly dancer." Contempt oiled Govan's voice. Still, he released the girl's hand, slapped her on the rump, and watched her scurry towards the safety of the musicians. "These performers are

advertised as genuine Darrians. I have a mind to have them arrested for fraud. I suspect ..." He ran the tip of his finger along his eating bowl. "They're mere Samilis."

Dahoud, himself a Samili, refused to react to the jab. Govan was not only satrap of the province, but Dahoud's employer, as well as the father of the lovely Esha.

"Samilis are everywhere these days." Peering down his nose, Govan swirled the wine in his beaker. "Not that I have anything against Samilis. Given the right kind of education, their race can develop remarkable intelligence, practically equal to that of Quislakis. They can make valuable contributions to society." He stroked the purple fringe of his armband, insignia of his rank. "Provided they respect their betters."

The other clerks at the table bobbed their chins in eager agreement.

Dahoud the Black Besieger would not have tolerated taunts from this pompous peacock, but Dahoud the council clerk had to bow. Submission was the price for guarding his secret.

ASSIGNMENT

In what way is your MC an 'underdog'? Identify at least one context, and think about how you can play this up early in the book.

Find a quick way to show the MC helping someone else in the first scene.

CHAPTER 6:
SEEN THROUGH THE EYES OF
PROFESSIONALS

To get to know your characters really well, put them under professional scrutiny.

Imagine professionals in different fields assessing your main character. Write a report from the perspective of a doctor, a financial adviser, a psychotherapist, an estate agent, a priest. What do they observe, speculate, comment on?

I suggest writing around three hundred words for each. At the end of this exercise, you'll know your MC in great depth.

THE DOCTOR

Imagine a doctor giving your MC a thorough examination. What are her observations and impressions?

How is the MC's general state of health? What old injuries does she observe? What's the state of his lungs, his joints, his teeth? What does she observe about his body weight and muscle mass? How are his blood-sugar level, his nutrition, his cardiovascular fitness? Are his health problems as bad as he thinks, are they mostly imagined, or are they worse? Does he suffer from an illness he's not yet aware of? What are her concerns about his lifestyle? What changes does she urge him to make?

Instead of a doctor, you can use the perspective of a homoeopath, faith healer, or other health professional if this suits the context of your story better.

THE ESTATE AGENT

Put yourself in the place of an estate agent (realtor) who assesses the MC before helping him find the right home.

What kind of home would suit this client? Rent or purchase? Villa or apartment? What price range? Family home or bachelor pad? Rural or urban? Lively location or quiet? What kind of neighbourhood? Near schools, near boutiques, near a railway station? How many rooms? Show home or fixer-upper? With garden, balcony or roof terrace? How realistic is the client about what he can afford? How confident is the estate agent that the rent or mortgage will be paid? What special considerations need to be taken into account – for example, wheelchair access for the MC's disabled mother, or a sound-proof cellar for his band's percussion practice?

THE PSYCHOTHERAPIST

If the MC were to attend a session (or course of sessions) with a psychologist, psychotherapist or counsellor, what would an expert think about the MC's emotional and mental state?

How self-aware is this person? What are his hang-ups, his inhibitions, his dreams, his fears? What secrets does he hide? What childhood traumas did he suffer, and how do they affect him now? What are his social skills like? His coping strategies? What is his default strategy for dealing with problems? What triggers cause emotional reactions? How healthy is his self-esteem? How healthy is his behaviour in relationships? Does he suffer from clinical depression, bi-polar disorder, schizophrenia, dissociation? Any addictions? Obsessions? Phobias? How well does the client cooperate during the consultation or treatment? What issues does the therapist feel should be addressed?

THE FINANCIAL ADVISER

Imagine a bank manager, underwriter, investment advisor or loan shark assessing the MC's finances.

Would she approve him for a loan – and if yes, to what amount, and with what collateral? If he's behind with loan repayments, what does she consider a practical solution? If he has money to invest, how much is it, and how would he like to see it invested – stocks and shares, real estate or government bonds? Low risk or high interest? Only environmentally sound companies, or only women-run enterprises? What are his current investments? What insurances does he have in place? Does she encourage him to spend less, or more? What does she consider the greatest risk for this client – his gambling habit, his lack of financial information, his poor judgement or his wife's profligate spending?

THE PRIEST

How would a priest (or rabbi, or other religious community leader) view this member of the flock?

Does the MC attend church every Sunday (mosque every Friday, synagogue on Saturday)? Or only at Christmas? Never? Does he attend every funeral service whether he knew the deceased or not? How genuine is his faith? How deep? How secure? Does he live his life according to the tenets of his faith – for example, does he obey the Ten Commandments and practice compassion? What are his sins? What are his greatest temptations? How knowledgeable is he about his religion – has he read the whole Bible once? Many times? Never? Only the juicy bits in the Old Testament? Only the excerpts he studied at school? Does he pay attention to sermons, does he nod off, does he secretly send text messages while the priest preaches? Besides the regular services, does he attend other faith-based events such as confession? Does he participate in the events of his religious community, such as fundraising tabletop sales? Does he volunteer for religious or social activities, such as teach Sunday School, tend the church garden, visit the sick? What's his attitude to religious leadership and hierarchy? How does he feel about other faiths?

If your MC is an atheist or agnostic and doesn't belong to any religious community, write the report from the perspective of a priest who hopes to covert him.

ASSIGNMENT

Write the 'professional' reports about your MC.

If you wish, you can repeat the exercise for other important characters, especially the antagonist and the love interest.

CHAPTER 7:
GIVE YOUR CHARACTER A SECRET

If your main character has a secret to hide, your novel will get more tension, and possibly more drama and depth, too.

WHAT IS THE SECRET?

It could be something in the MC's past – perhaps an atrocious crime she committed in her youth, of which she was never suspected and which she regrets deeply but which, if found out, would ruin her reputation, her career, her marriage, perhaps lead to imprisonment. Maybe she did something careless or foolish – drunk driving, playing a silly prank – which killed her friend's mother, and the friend would never forgive that.

During an interview, she might have claimed more experience than she had in order to land a temporary job. It's only for two months, and as long as she can do the job, who cares? Two months from now, it will all be over and the fib will be forgotten, won't it?

Perhaps she didn't do anything wrong, but thinks it best to keep the truth to herself. Here's an example.

A modern young woman has a one-night stand. She and the man are both single, consenting and in agreement that they don't want to take it beyond that one encounter. Then she discovers that she's pregnant, and decides to raise the child alone. Normally, a woman would name the child's father on the birth certificate, and get financial support from him. But the man has subsequently married – the MC's beloved sister! He doesn't even recognise the MC as the woman from his casual encounter, and he's devoted to his new wife.

Rather than cause her sister pain and put a strain on her marriage, the MC decides to 'forget' who the father is. Since her concerned sister probes for details, the MC even invents a few details about the man, as different from the real father as possible. It's better for everyone, isn't it?

WHY IS THIS SO TERRIBLE?

The secret may have started out as a small fib, a white lie, or even a misunderstanding the MC didn't immediately correct. But it has grown.

The woman who secured a two-month temp job performs so well that she gets hired permanently. Now she has to fill in forms about her employment history. Since she can't admit that she lied during the interview, she now repeats her claims in writing, inventing details that will look real.

Three years later, she's her department's star performer, and the best candidate for promotion to manager – but only if her employers don't find out that she has lied to them all the time. So she lies some more, even obtains a fake reference. Ten years on, she is managing director of the company, and spearheading a campaign for truth and honesty. Someone – a determined reporter, or a disgruntled ex-employee she sacked for dishonesty – notices that details in her background don't add up, and investigates...

The single mum who declined to name her baby's father is happy with her decision... until her daughter grows up and falls in love with her sister's son, not realising that he's her half-brother. The MC tries everything to discourage the relationship. She forbids her daughter to date him, saying he's unsuitable for her (her sister takes umbrage at that). She even moves to another part of the country and takes her teenage daughter with her, hoping she'll forget the boy. But they keep corresponding, and when she's eighteen, they announce their engagement. The MC has to stop this marriage – but how? If she belatedly reveals the truth, her sister will never forgive her the nineteen years of lies. Moreover, her sister's marriage is going through a rough patch, and the revelation could prove the breaking point.

The secret may be small or forgivable at the beginning – but it grows into a terrible monster.

WHAT WOULD BE THE CONSEQUENCES IF FOUND OUT?

Raise the stakes and make the consequences devastating. If found out, the MC would lose her freedom, her job, her reputation, her wealth, her health, her children, or her marriage.

HOW DOES THE MC FEEL ABOUT THE SECRET?

Does she feel guilt or shame about what she has done, or both, or neither? How does it affect her self-image?

How does she feel about having to live a lie?

WHOSE SECRET IS IT?

Perhaps the MC is keeping someone else's secret rather than her own. She cover up her brother's desertion from the army, or denies knowledge of the whereabouts of a Jewish family during the holocaust in Nazi Germany.

HOW DOES THE MC PRESERVE THE SECRET?

What actions does the MC take to conceal the truth? Here are some ideas to get your imagination going. Notice how they vary in severity. They may start mild and get worse.

- She evades the subject
- If anyone asks probing questions, she simply gives them a superior smile
- She instructs her publicist to reply 'no comment' when a certain topic gets raised
- When someone accuses her, she turns the tables and accuses them back
- When challenged, she denies everything
- She buys the silence of people in the know

- She makes sure she holds some kind of power over anyone who might reveal something
- She tells lies
- She falsifies documents
- She uses image manipulation to create photos and posts them in the social media
- She pays for false witnesses
- She swears a false oath
- When someone from the past turns up, she implies that their memory is faulty (early onset Alzheimer's perhaps)
- When challenged, she laughs off the accusations

HOW DOES THE SECRET ESCALATE?

It may have started in such a small, harmless way. Let's say she happens to be walking on the beach in stormy weather when she finds the unconscious body of a small boy. She bends over him, wondering what kind of first aid to give, when he wakes and vomits water.

More people come by gather round the scene, speculate what has happened. One says: "This young lady pulled the boy out of the water." Another comments: "That was a brave thing to do, in this storm. She might have drowned herself."

Although she says, "I didn't actually do much, I was just trying to resuscitate him," people keep telling one another about her supposed bravery. She doesn't bother contradicting them.

Then the boy's parents come, and thank her. "It's not what you think, I haven't done much," she says, but they wave this off as excessive modesty.

When the local newspaper publishes an article about her as the daring heroine, she might ask them to print a correction, but she enjoys the appreciation of her neighbours too much. When the boy's wealthy parents offer to fund her college tuition in gratitude, she accepts.

Things get more complicated when a famous blogger interviews her for a post about courageous women – now she has to make up details. And then the local Women's Institute invites her to give a talk about the experience. She invents even more.

She gets invited to dinner with the mayor and local celebrities, and enjoys that fame very much – especially since she has a crush on the mayor and he's getting interested in her.

Next, she gets asked to represent the town in a national event – a celebrity swimming gala. The famous rescuer will be the town's champion! Oh dear! She can't actually swim – but to admit that would be as good as a confession that she didn't rescue the drowning boy. Goodbye admiration from neighbours, goodbye reputation, goodbye college fees, goodbye handsome mayor! She can't give all that up – not now that she's about to get her degree, and the mayor is on the brink of proposing marriage!

So she takes beginner swimming lessons – and she has to do this in secret. Even the instructor must not know who she is! But the swimming pool attendant suspects. He films her covertly and threatens to publish the videos on YouTube unless she pays up. Now she has to deal with blackmail...

You can have fun escalating this further and further.

MAKE SURE THE READER UNDERSTANDS THE MOTIVATION

If the story takes place in a different period or a society with different values, the reader may not comprehend why the MC doesn't simply come out with the truth.

Let's say the MC lost her virginity when she was eighteen and succumbed to the wiles of a notorious womaniser who didn't even hang around for breakfast.

To the modern reader, this isn't a big issue. So what if she's not a virgin? Many unmarried women in the western world aren't. The girl should simply forget about the encounter and move on. It's certainly not worth spinning an elaborate network of deception around this. Even if her future betrothed expects his fiancée to be a virgin, she can simply come clean, and if he's a good man, he'll forgive her mistake.

But to young lady in the upper classes of Regency England around Jane Austen's time, the loss of virginity – if it became known – meant her ruin. She lost her prospects of marriage, which in those days was a woman's purpose and livelihood. The few options an upper class female had of honourable employment would also be barred to her, because nobody would engage a companion or governess with a tarnished reputation. Her parents' standing in society would suffer, and her sisters' chances of a good marriage would shrink too.

Make sure the reader fully grasps what the consequences would be – for example, by having characters talk about a fallen woman, or declining to speak about a disowned relative.

THREATEN EXPOSURE

Throughout the book, hint at several ways how the secret might come to light by accident or malice. The MC is aware of the dangers, and the reader worries with her. If someone discovers those old diaries... if the tourists post their snapshots on Twitter... if Bill is disgruntled and reveals what he knows... if Suzie gets drunk and blurts out the truth... if a civil servant demands to see the marriage certificate.... Put several possibilities in the reader's mind. This will increase the suspense.

REVEALING THE SECRET

If possible, make it the MC's choice to tell the truth.

After hiding the secret for so long, near the end of the book, she summons the courage and comes out.

Give her a compelling reason to tell the truth even though it means she will lose her reputation, her wealth, her position in society, or whatever she has fought to protect.

To whom does she come out – only to the one person who matters, or to the public? How? What are the reactions? Write that scene. It doesn't need to be long, but it should be detailed and tense. The best place for the big confession is probably in the final third of the book, perhaps immediately before the climax.

If you like, you can reveal the secret bit by bit. Perhaps parts of it come out in earlier chapters – by accident, malice or confession – but the full truth is revealed only at the climax.

OTHER CHARACTERS CAN HAVE SECRETS, TOO

Beside the MC, other major characters can have secrets, too, especially the antagonist and the love interest.

Depending on the novel's genre, length and complexity, even some minor characters may have secrets. For example, in mysteries and thrillers, witnesses try to cover up a secret that's unrelated to the crime, and their evasions make them suspect.

While it's best to delay the exposure of the MC's secret until near the novel's end, other characters' secrets can come out sooner, perhaps due to the MC's diligent investigation.

FROM MY PERSONAL EXPERIENCE

Characters may keep their secrets even from the author. **Dahoud** kept his for a long time. I'd written almost a whole novel before he confessed that he was possessed by a demon, and then he mentioned it to me in such a casual way that I nearly missed it.

After I'd rewritten the whole book, he mentioned that he'd been a general, and that he'd brutally devastated a whole region.. but he didn't admit which region. It took another rewrite before he confessed that the region he had once devastated was the place he was supposed to rule! This put an entirely new spin on things. If his subjects realised who he was, they'd tear him to pieces alive.

Dahoud went to great lengths to conceal his past: he even faked his own death, allegedly at the hands of an enraged woman, with a funeral pyre and everything. Then he lived the lowly life of a labourer, stirring pots of boiling piss for textile dyers and lugging bricks for builders, and swallowing the humiliating taunts of pompous bureaucrats.

Once I knew these secrets, I helped Dahoud keep them, and I also created many situations where they almost came out. The frequent threats created enormous tension. In the run-up to the book's climax, Dahoud reveals the demon to Merida, and his role in the region's brutal devastation to his honourable rival, Mansour.

Merida assured me that she was so honest she would never hide anything from anyone. She spoke the truth.

Devious author that I am, I threw her into plot situations where she had no choice but to keep secrets. Locked up in the harem, she had to conceal her escape plans, acting as if she was submitting to her fate.

Then she had to pretend to be a tavern belly dancer, actually putting on a show in a tavern, with Dahoud in the audience. I had great fun writing those scenes, pitting the wits of Dahoud and Merida against each other. Dahoud really needed to find and capture the escaped concubine, or his friends would die. Merida really needed to hide her identity, or her freedom would be forfeit. Fans tell me these scenes are their favourite part of *Storm Dancer.*

Tarkan's big secret is that he's gay. In a homophobic society, where 'men-lovers' are put to death by drowning (or used as targets for knife-throwing practice), nobody must find out, or his life wouldn't be worth a fig. Throughout the novel, he acted straight, flirting with females, pretending to be in love with women who were married and therefore unavailable. Although several people suspected his orientation and some even framed him, I allowed Tarkan to keep his secret. Those close to him came to accept it, but the public still don't know – especially since Tarkan entered a marriage of convenience with a woman who has secrets of her own.

ASSIGNMENT

What is your main character's secret?

What would the devastating consequences be if it came out?

How did it begin? How does it escalate?

What does she do to guard the secret? (List several measures she takes.)

In what ways might the secret be threatened? (Think of several possibilities.)

When, how, and to whom does she tell the truth?

CHAPTER 8:
HOW DOES THE CHARACTER REACT TO PROBLEMS?

Fiction characters meet a lot of problems – from minor setbacks to devastating disasters, from half-expected obstacles to shocking surprises.

Everyone reacts to troubles in a different way, and has their own approach to problem-solving. What is this character's default mode? When faced with a worrying issue, what's her immediate response? After she's had time to think, how does she face the challenge?

Decide this for every important character in the book – the MC and all the major characters.

Here's a list of ideas to get you started.

When disaster strikes, the character...

… cuddles her teddy

… calls her mum

… curses

… prays

… yells

… cries

… eats three big bars of chocolate

… trusts her husband to solve the problem

… downs a double whisky

… ignores the problem, pretending it doesn't exist

… keeps herself busy with other matters

… researches the issue on the internet

… buys a book on the subject

… hires an expert to deal with the issue

… berates herself for being so stupid

… blames the messenger

… finds others to blame

… considers how this will affect her status or reputation

… worries how much this is going to cost

… goes to the gym for a vigorous workout

… punches a sandbag

… beats up her children

… has her slaves whipped

… treats herself to a new pair of shoes

… stays in bed

… goes to the pub, drowns her sorrows in beer

… has sex with the first person available

… finds a way to pass the problem to someone else

… sits down with pen and paper and brainstorms solutions

… creates structured charts for problem-solving

… writes a list of ten possible ways to deal with the problem, then chooses the best

… calls her team for an emergency meeting

… books an appointment with her therapist

… throws something against a wall

… does vigorous digging and weeding in her garden

… cleans her kitchen and scrubs her floors until they're spotless

… meditates

… recalls previous experiences and applies what she learnt from those

… considers who she knows who can advise her

… joins an internet forum on the topic and posts a request for advice

... follows the rules and established procedures

... procrastinates

… gives up her big plan, because it was obviously not meant to be

… pours out her troubles to her best friend who is a good listener

… puts on her favourite music at loud volume and dances wildly

… withdraws into her art and pours out her anger, worry and confusion onto the canvas

… goes for a long walk, regardless of the weather

FROM MY PERSONAL EXPERIENCE

Storm Dancer is a big book, and my main characters meet many challenges. Here are some of my characters' default reactions:

Dahoud immediately takes charge when he faces a problem. He assesses the problem systematically and draws on his past experience as a siege commander to decide what is best.

Merida's default is to follow established rules and procedures. When those don't apply, she practices martial arts drills to focus her mind. Then she researches the topic, develops a comprehensive plan and prepares thoroughly. I had fun putting her in situations where established procedures didn't apply, and where she had to act without time for research, planning or preparation. We authors are such devious people!

Whatever terror and turmoil strike at **Tarkan's** heart, he chooses to stay serene and courteous, as if the problem doesn't affect him. He uses diplomacy to get out of difficult situations.

ASSIGNMENT

Choose your MC's default reaction on discovering problems, and her approach to solving them.

Do the same for other important characters, especially the antagonist and the love interest. Don't bother with the minor characters – those won't experience enough problems in the book.

CHAPTER 9:
CHOOSING NAMES

Names can reveal a lot about characters, so choose them carefully. But don't rush to look up on the internet what would be an appropriate name for a pure meek woman, for a romantic nerdy man or a sadistic evil villain. That would lead to stereotyped characters.

FIRST NAMES

The first name (also referred to as the 'given name' or 'Christian name') normally gets chosen by the parents, and they choose it before they know what the child is like, often even before the child is born.

This name therefore reveals nothing about the character's personality, and a lot about the parents' tastes, hopes and aspirations.

Consider the name 'Agnes' which means 'pure'. Agnes's parent may have chosen the name because they hoped for a chaste, gentle, meek daughter – which doesn't mean she turned out that way. Agnes may be passionate, abrasive and bold. You can have fun presenting a character whose personality is at odds with her parents' expectations.

The name choice may also have familial, social, religious or even political reasons. Maybe it's a family tradition to name the first-born daughter Agnes, or perhaps the parents named her after a wealthy aunt in hopes that the girl would be chosen as heiress to the fortune. If the parents were pious Catholics, they may have named the girl born on 21 January Agnes because in the Catholic calendar, that's St. Agnes's day.

A character's first name can give the reader an instant clue about his origins: Duncan and Geillis are probably (though not necessarily) Scots, Rajiv and Pratima Indians, Sergej and Svetlana Russians. First names can also indicate a religious group: Mohammed and Fatima are probably Muslims, while Krishna and Parvati are Hindus.

Sometimes, a character may legally change her first name. Perhaps she hates her parents' choice (and really doesn't wish to go through the rest of her life called Fifipuss or Hashtag), or she changed her religion, so the name Christiane or Lakshmi is no longer appropriate, or perhaps she feels that her obviously ethnic name hampers her career prospects, so she changes from Abimbola to Jane.

Depending on the country, a name change involves a lengthy and costly legal process and it's not something undertaken lightly. Consider her motivation: it reveals a lot about her values and self-image.

SHORT FORMS OF FIRST NAMES

While the full first name reveals little or nothing about the character's personality, the short version does. How do the character's friends and colleagues address her?

Let's say her first name is Patricia, a name which can be shortened in myriad ways. People who know her well will inevitably pick the version they feel suits her best. Do they call her Patricia? Or Pat, Patty, Patsy, Trisha, Trish, Ricia...?

Do Robert's friends call him Robert, Rob, Bob, Bobby or Bert? Is Richard Richard, or Rich, Rick, Dickon or Dick?

If you're unsure, simply ask the other characters what they call her.

How does the character feel about this short form? Is it what she would have chosen for herself? Her reaction can be revealing.

Years ago, I worked with a colleague named Patricia whom everyone called Pat – and she hated it! She insisted on being called Patricia – an interesting contrast between how others perceived her and how she saw herself.

NICKNAMES

Nicknames are hugely revealing. They may be variants of the first or family name, teasing comments on the character's personality or looks, or references to a childhood incident. Some nicknames are used by everyone, others only by family or close friends.

How does the character feel about her nickname? Does she love it, accept it or hate it? If she dislikes it, do people use it anyway? Why?

SURNAMES

The surname (also referred to as 'family' name) comes from the parents – either father or mother or both, depending on the culture. It reveals little about the personality, but can convey clues about the character's geographic or ethnic background.

A character surnamed Campbell or Mackintosh has probably Scots ancestry, while Blutstein or Rosenzweig may indicate German Jews, and there's a good chance that someone with the surname Vella or Azzopardi hails from Malta, or her ancestors did.

MIX UP THE NAMES

Make the names for your characters as different as possible, to avoid confusing readers. If you have characters named Jane, June, Jean, Jan, Joan and Jeanine, readers will get confused about who is who.

Vary the first letters especially, so your cast of characters doesn't consist of Ally, Adam, Abel, Aram, Amanda, Agnes, Arthur, Alex, Ariel and Abdul.

Vary the length of names as well, so that some names have a single syllable, others two, three, four or five. For readability, give the MC and the major characters relatively short names, and keep the polysyllabic names for minor characters.

FROM MY PERSONAL EXPERIENCE

After I finished the second draft of *Storm Dancer,* I compiled a list of names and discovered that most characters had names starting with D, M, or T!

In the novel's climax section, several scenes pitched the MC Dahoud against his adversary Darryush, and the constant 'Da.../Da...' made awkward reading. That's why Darryush became Baryush.

I kept Dahoud, Marida, Mansour, Tarkan and Teruma, but changed the names of everyone else.

ASSIGNMENT

Make two lists for the characters' names in your novel: one for the names you'll definitely use, and one for those where you're still undecided.

Play with the names in the second list until all names are as different from one another as you can make them.

CHAPTER 10:
DESCRIBING PEOPLE

By sketching a quick portrait in words, you can bring characters to life for your readers – but you can also bore your readers and encourage them to skip paragraphs. Here are some professional techniques you may want to use.

1. Keep Descriptions Short

Keep character descriptions short, but meaningful. Readers don't really want to know all the minutiae of what a character looks like and wears. Pick a few relevant details, and allow the reader's imagination to fill in the rest of the picture.

2. Show Personality

Choose details which reveal something about the character's personality, background or personality. Instead of informing the reader about the colour of the eyes, let them see the bitten fingernails, broken front tooth or frayed cufflinks.

3. Describe the First Encounter

The best time to describe a character is when she makes her first appearance in the book, or if a PoV character encounters her for the first time. That's when a quick pen sketch helps convey a first impression.

4. Use Similes to Create First Impressions

You can sum up what a person looks like by giving not details, but overall impressions. Use a creative simile for this, perhaps using 'like' or 'as if' to compare the character with someone or something else.

Here are some examples:

Her face had a stern pinched look, as if she saw everything in the world and approved of nothing.

He looked like a man who spent more time in the gym than in the office.

She had the well-kept appearance of a woman with time to spend on Pilates and pedicures.

5. Show Teeth

If you can fit it smoothly into the scene, mention what the character's teeth look like. Teeth can reveal a lot about hygiene habits, access to dental care and lifestyle. Are the teeth immaculate works of the dental surgeon's art? Are they sparkling white, stained, nicotine-yellowed, broken? Are any teeth missing?

The best time to show a character's teeth is when he smiles or grins.

6. Show Hands

A few words about a character's hands convey something about his lifestyle: are they manicured, wrinkled, blistered, dirt-smeared, paint-stained, calloused? Are the fingers slender, elegant, chubby, gnarled? What about the nails: manicured, clean, varnished, short, long, broken, black-rimmed? Is the nail varnish applied with professional skill, smudged on the fingers, or chipped?

Describe the hands the first time the PoV character (or the reader) has the opportunity to observe them.

7. Tone of Voice

Describe what the character's voice sounds like: is it squeaky, hoarse, deep, high-pitched, gravelly, suave? Does the character have a stutter, a speech impediment, a regional accent? Consider using a simile, comparing the voice to something else.

The best time to describe the voice is in a dialogue scene, immediately after she has said something.

Here are two examples:

"Of course I would be delighted." The geisha's voice tinkled like a temple bell.

"Tomorrow we'll know for sure." He spoke in the deep, resonant voice of a trained stage actor.

8. Include Smells

An effective way to describe a character in just a few words is to mention what he smells like. A single sentence about smells creates a more vivid picture in the reader's mind than a whole paragraph of visuals.

Do this the first time the PoV character gets close to that person.

Here are some examples:

He smelled of nicotine, pizza and stale sweat.

She smelled of patchouli and incense.

He smelled of leather, horses and wood smoke.

She smelled of coal mouthwash, mothballs and coal tar soap.

9. The Character Moves

Weave hints about the character's appearance into his actions, letting his movements imply his age, body shape and level of fitness.

Compare these two sentences:

John heaved himself out of the chair. (The reader sees a big, heavy man, not very fit.)

John tottered across the room. (The reader sees a frail, elderly man.)

John marched across the room. (The reader sees a strong, energetic man of military bearing.)

10. Show Clothes

What does the character wear? Don't waste words describing every garment. Instead, pick one or two items and let the choice of clothes reveal something about the character's personality, lifestyle and taste.

Does he wear an Armani shirt with silver cufflinks, or a crumpled shirt with the name of his favourite football team? Is her blouse high-necked and tight-buttoned or figure-hugging and cleavage-revealing?

Shoes are a good indicator, too: buffed or scuffed? Worn-down heels? Unevenly tied?

11. Use Vivid Verbs

People descriptions can feel static, and this bores the reader. Bring them to life by replacing the dull verbs *be (was/were), have, seem,* and *wear* with vivid verbs. Here are some examples.

Instead of:

There were ketchup stains on his shirt front.

Write:

Ketchup stains blotched his shirt front.

Instead of:

There was a mole on the bridge of her nose.

Write:

A mole perched on the bridge of her nose.

Instead of:

She was slender and wore a wide swinging skirt.

Write:

A wide skirt swung around her slender legs.

12. Filtering Descriptions through the PoV

Does your scene have a Point-of-View character? Then describe other people through the filter of her perceptions – the way she sees them, not the way you the author do.

Different people will perceive different things. Let's say fashion-conscious Mary and her fourteen-year-old son John meet their new neighbour, Mrs Smith.

If you write the scene from Mary's point of view, you might write:

Mrs Smith's long-line cardigan failed to conceal her ample curves.

From John's point of view, however, the description might be more like this:

Mrs Smith had the biggest boobs he'd ever seen outside the internet.

13. Describing the PoV Character

The PoV can't see herself unless she gazes into the mirror. So how do you show what she looks like?

Many novice writers agonise about this, but experienced authors don't worry. Readers don't care what colour the PoV character's eyes are, they want to know what she does and feels. All they need is a few clues about her general appearance.

You can weave clues into the action, preferably early in the story.

Here are some examples of how to hint that the PoV character is big, tall or short respectively:

Mary squeezed through the gate.

Mary ducked through the gate.

Mary stood on her toes to undo the gate latch.

A brief mention of why a character chooses to wear certain clothes can fill the reader in about the looks:

Mary decided to wear the kimono which emphasised her Asian features.

Mary slipped into her baggy black trousers which would hide her bulges.

John decided to wear the brown lace-ups with insets which gave him an extra inch of height.

A few scattered hints are enough. Readers don't need to see the PoV character in detail, because if you write the story well, they become the character and experience the story through her.

If you're interested in learning more about Point-of-View techniques, you may want to read my book *Writing Deep Point of View.*

PROFESSIONAL EXAMPLES

Take a peek at how the masters handle people descriptions, and see if you can spot any of the techniques I've described above:

Rain beat very hard against the windows. They were shut tight and it was hot in the room and I had a little fan going on the table. The breeze from it hit Dravec's face high up, lifted his heavy black hair, moved the longer bristles in the fat path of eyebrow that went across his face in a solid line. He looked like a bouncer who had come into money.

He showed me some of his gold teeth and said: "What you got on me?"

(Raymond Chandler, *Killer in the Rain*)

Fifty years of age. Expensive hair, even more expensive loungewear. The kind of well-kept woman who spends her days doing a lot of yoga and not much else.

(Lisa Gardner, *3 Truths and a Lie*)

Eve Ward was sitting close against one wall, flesh loose on the bones of her face, lipstick bravely rather than wisely applied, her hair hennaed and roughly combed. She was wearing a dark wool coat that had seen better days and, beneath it, a mauve cardigan fastened with a safety pin. Chipped red polish on her nails.

(John Harvey: *Darkness & Light*)

It wasn't long before the answer lurched through the morgue doors, hauling at the crotch of her SOC coveralls and coughing as if she was about to bring up a lung. DI Steel, their senior investigating officer. A five-foot-nine, wrinkly, middle-aged disaster area, smelling of stale cigarette smoke and Chanel Number Five.

(Stuart McBride, *Broken Skin*)

The proprietor-cum-chef is a gnarled ancient wearing a greasy, gold-embroidered skull-cap, a henna-streaked grey beard and three long, protruding brown teeth in the left corner of his mouth.

(Dervla Murphy, *Where the Indus Is Young*)

FROM MY PERSONAL EXPERIENCE

Since Dahoud is the main character in *Storm Dancer*, and the PoV of most chapters, I didn't describe his looks. My plan was to leave this to each reader's imagination.

However, the team of artists who painted the book cover wanted a description. That's when I asked fifty or so readers who had read the book to describe what they imagined Dahoud to look like. To my surprise, they largely agreed on Dahoud's appearance, even though I had not described it in the book.

"Like a young Joe Manganiello," several said.

I had imagined him to be more ordinary looking... but since the hot handsome hero on the cover sells the book, I'm not complaining. The artwork was a collaboration between Paul Davies and Erica Syverson. Here's the link to the book cover on Amazon: myBook.to/ SD

Actually, there is one brief (and fairly vague) description, from Merida's PoV. She's in disguise as a whiteseer when she meets Dahoud for the first time.

Suddenly the air sang with danger. A rider vaulted off his grey horse. The sight of his moss-green tunic and plaited belt hit her guts. This was one of the Consort's henchmen, a thousand miles from the palace. Had he come to arrest her?

She took a step back, poised for flight.

"A reading, please, seer." His voice was deep like a slow-flowing river, smooth on top but dangerous beneath.

She allowed herself to meet his eyes, as if she had nothing to fear from his kind. Although his mouth smiled, his eyes were bitter-dark like olives. An aura of vibrant intelligence was enveloped in intense bitterness, and under his cheerful courtesy, pain radiated from him like heat searing from a fire.

Her instincts screamed at her to pull free from the dangerous power before it could burn her, but a genuine wandering seer would not

panic at the sight of a palace official, and bolting would draw his suspicion.

She forced herself to stay in her role. "Your hands," she demanded, careful to hide her accent.

The hands were wrong. Brown, with short dirty nails, calloused, rough and ridged with old scars, they did not belong to a courtier, nor even to a guard.

ASSIGNMENT

Choose a scene where two characters in your novel meet for the first time.

Describe one of them through the filter of the other's (PoV character's) experience. Focus on a few telling details, choosing from techniques suggested in this chapter.

CHAPTER 11:
SIDEKICKS, LIEUTENANTS, CONFIDANTS AND MINIONS

In your novel, the protagonist and antagonist probably have several supporters each, and some of these can play an important role in the plot.

SIDEKICK

The sidekick is a major character who tends to stick close to the main character (or to the antagonist, as the case may be).

His personality differs from the MC's and complements it. Is the MC introverted, tone-deaf and modest? Then the sidekick can be an extrovert, musical braggart. If you give your sidekick personality quirks, you can create comedic effects or light relief during the story's darkest stretches.

Often, the sidekick has an unsavoury past. He may have served a jail sentence for breaking and entering, or he may be hiding from four deserted and enraged ex-wives.

Give the sidekick an unusual skill – one the MC doesn't have – and employ it as part of the plot. Does he excel at tightrope-walking, wine tasting or poker? Show this casually in several scenes before the sidekick applies it to save the day.

The honourable MC may feel ambivalent about this skill and perhaps even disapprove. Maybe she objects to his poker-playing on moral grounds, and constantly worries that he may fall back into his old habit of picking pockets or burglary. But in the critical moment when all seems lost, he outwits the villain's henchman in a game of poker, steals back the purloined jewel or breaks the lock to the MC's prison cell.

The sidekick is loyal to the MC, often uncritically. Give him a compelling reason for this loyalty. Is it hero worship? Gratitude? A family bond?

Protagonist and antagonist usually have only one sidekick each. Other supporting characters may be lieutenants, confidants or minions. In some novels, the sidekick is an animal. A dog is perfect for this role because of its intelligence and loyal nature.

LIEUTENANT

This is a major or minor character who has the authority to act on the MC's (or antagonist's, or sometimes other major character's) behalf. He may be her agent, her housekeeper, a senior officer in her army, a sergeant where she is an inspector, a deputy where she is a sheriff.

He is intelligent, has leadership skills, possesses the MC's trust, and holds a position of responsibility.

A major character may have more than one lieutenant, although not all of them play a major role in the book.

The lieutenant's motives are interesting. Why did he take this job? Was it a career move, did he feel passionate about working for the cause, or did he join because he admired the MC?

Part of the plot can revolve around a lieutenant's loyalty. What if the villain's lieutenant realises that he's been fighting for evil, and switches sides? What if the antagonist recruits the MC's lieutenant with a higher wage and better benefits? What if the lieutenant's loyalties are divided – on the one hand he is committed to the cause, on the other hand he's in love with the antagonist's daughter? What if the MC's trusted lieutenant turns out to be a spy in the service of the enemy? What if he is loyal, but someone else sows seeds of distrust in the MC's mind? What if his main loyalty is to the cause, and he feels the MC has betrayed the cause? What if he is ambitious, secretly believes he could do a better job than the MC, and plans to supplant her?

CONFIDANT

This is an important character, especially in romance novels, where he serves as the MC's sounding board, advisor and conscience. The dialogue between the MC and the confidant enables you to share the MC's thoughts and feelings in a lively way.

The confidant is honest, outspoken, and has the MC's best interests at heart. He may or may not be right, but his opinions are worth considering. Whether or not the MC takes his advice, she gains a wider perspective and a deeper understanding of the situation.

In a long novel, you can weave a subplot around this character, ideally something related to the main plot. Perhaps he experiences a different facet of the MC's motivation or dilemma. While the MC seeks her birth mother, he tries to adopt a child. While the MC grieves for the recent death of her parents, he cares for his dying grandfather.

The word 'confidant' is sometimes spelled 'confidante', and there's no consensus about which is right in which context.

SAMURAI

Inspired by the movie *The Seven Samurai*, this term describes an important team member. Several characters set out to achieve a goal – capture a castle, find a hidden artefact, hunt down a serial killer – and each brings his own skills, strengths and weaknesses to the quest. The main character is usually, but not always, the team's leader.

The first part of the plot often revolves around the leader recruiting her team before they go off on their adventure. This structure is popular in the movies *(The Seven Samurai, The Dirty Dozen, The Magnificent Seven etc.)* and also in myths *(Jason and the Argonauts, King Arthur and the Knights of the Round Table).*

The challenge is to make each member of the team a distinct character, so readers won't confuse them. Give them different ages, genders, ethnicities, backgrounds, ranks, body shapes, strengths and weaknesses. For increased diversity, you may want to include characters with physical disabilities. The individuals' limitations and prejudices can create interesting challenges and tensions.

Aim for as much diversity as your plot allows, but don't let political correctness outweigh plausibility. A black African character is unlikely to participate in a Viking expedition in the 8th century, and a wheelchair user probably won't join a three-month jungle trek.

MINION

Minions are minor characters (sometimes mere spear-carriers – see Chapter 2) who support the MC, the antagonist or another important character.

They have no authority and little responsibility. They may or may not be loyal to their leader or the cause. Often, they are hirelings – mercenaries, grunt soldiers, low-paid staff.

If they play a role in the plot, it is often as a group rather than as individuals, and their actions are triggered by how their employer treats them. Does she pay them a good wage, praise them for a job well done, take an interest in their welfare? Then they'll work conscientiously and reject bribes. Does she keep them in chains, abuse them verbally, punish them for the smallest error? Then they'll perform their duties perfunctorily and desert at the first opportunity.

FROM MY PERSONAL EXPERIENCE

In *Storm Dancer,* some sidekicks attached themselves to major characters uninvited. **Yora,** a spunky, courageous, resourceful young girl was always looking for a strong leader to follow (and subconsciously for a parent figure), so she attached herself first to Mansour, then to Dahoud, and finally to Merida. They found her a hindrance at first, but soon discovered how useful it was to have this spunky girl around.

Haurvatat is another character who attached herself uninvited. Unhappy, weak and lonely, this harem inmate was drawn to Merida's strength and energy and tried to become her confidant. Unfortunately for her, Merida was looking for intellectual companionship and otherwise wanted to be left alone.

Idrahad is a typical lieutenant, the right-hand man of the local chieftain Mansour. He resents Dahoud, who is Mansour's major rival for power.

ASSIGNMENT

Do you have supporting characters in the novel you're working on? If yes, what are they – confidants, lieutenants, sidekicks, samurai or minions? If not, consider whether one of the major or minor characters could take on this function.

CHAPTER 12:
ANIMAL CHARACTERS

Readers love animals. Some authors report that they get more fan mail about the hero's dog than about the hero, and several publishers have told me that novel series sell best if they have a recurring animal character.

Could you include an animal in your story? Maybe the MC could have a canine or feline sidekick. Perhaps the MC's love interest is devoted to her horse, or the villain has a close bond with his dog.

If possible, choose the kind of animal of which you have personal experience. Do you have a cat, a dog, a snake, a raven? Then you can write about it with authenticity. If you get it right, animal lovers will smile in recognition.

If you need to research an animal, opt for an unusual pet – how about a goat, a donkey, a fox? Talk to owners and try to get some hands-on experience.

Make the animal realistic, otherwise your readers will write scathing reviews and letters of complaint. The dog should behave like a dog, the cat like a cat, and the camel like a camel. Consider the animal's natural skills and weaknesses. Use them for realism and to drive parts of the plot.

Let's take a cat, for example. Cats can jump from great heights without getting hurt, and have excellent eyesight even when there's little light. However, they have relatively few taste buds and don't see colours well. In your story, the cat may leap from the third storey when the human MC can't, and find an escape route in the darkness of the night. But the plot had better not hinge on the cat detecting a flavour difference between two ice creams, or picking the correct nuance of green.

If the animal in your story has skills not common to the species, keep them realistic. Check that it's something the animal can physically do. Perhaps Tommy the Cat is able to open doors by pressing the handle down – a rare but occasionally heard-of skill. However, he won't be able to insert and turn a key because for that he would need opposable thumbs.

In its natural habitat, is the animal a predator or prey? This will affect its behaviour in the plot. A cat is a predator, so it may stalk, pounce and attack, and only occasionally hide under the couch for safety. A rabbit, on the other hand, will always flee.

Daily and seasonal rhythms affect the animal's behaviour. Bears hibernate in winter, and you can use the bear coming out of winter sleep as part of the plot. Cats sleep around seventeen hours daily, and are often awake at night when their human snores. Perhaps the cat becomes aware of a night time intruder or a fire in the building and alerts the sleeping human just in time. Dawn and dusk are the times when cats' hunting instincts are strongest, and you may be able to build this into the plot.

Many animals' behaviour is triggered by temperature, and they may become sluggish on cold winter days or during the noon heat. Some reptiles are inactive and stiff while it's cold, but suddenly come to life when it gets warm – an effect you may be able to use in your story.

Every kind of animal has different senses. Many rely on their sense of smell to a much greater extent than humans do, and their behaviour needs to reflect this. Some can hear far better than we do, perceive a wider spectrum of colours, or distinguish between flavours of which we are not aware. Some animals are equipped with additional senses, for example, a homing pigeon's ability to know in which direction to fly.

What does the animal fear? This can create interesting plot complications. Most animals fear fire, though they can overcome their dread if there's a compelling motivation, such as a tasty human sitting by the campfire. The majority of cats will run from water – but some enjoy bathing and swimming. Elephants flee from sudden noise.

When writing a Thriller, Horror or Adventure story, consider how the animal will react to the smell of blood. A lion will be attracted, a horse terrified.

Make the animal typical of its species – but at the same time, present it as an individual character. This is best achieved by blending 'normal' behaviour with quirks. A cat character, for example, may be fond of sleeping in cardboard boxes, lying on keyboards when the human wants to type, playing with ribbons and eating fish – many felines do, and cat lovers will smile in recognition. At the same time, your fictional cat needs individual quirks: maybe Tommy the Cat loves to drink coffee and adores the smell of female human feet, which can lead to funny situations when he sips from visitors' cups and sniffs ecstatically at their open-toe sandals.

A big question to consider is how much to anthropomorphise the animal, that is, give it human attitudes. My advice: anthropomorphise as little as possible, and as much as the story needs. An animal that appears to think and reason like a human evokes smiles and laughter – but this works better for internet memes than for fiction characters. In a novel, it's usually best if the animal thinks, feels and behaves in keeping with its species.

In fantasy fiction, the animal can have a human attribute or paranormal ability, but it's best to stick to just one. Fantasy readers are willing to suspend their disbelief if Tommy the Cat can talk human, but they won't believe it if he also cooks breakfast and solves crosswords.

FROM MY PERSONAL EXPERIENCE

In *Storm Dancer*, I tried to give Dahoud an equine sidekick, but soon realised that I simply didn't know enough about horses to pull this off. Although I sought advice from horse experts, Dahoud's silver mare just didn't develop into a fully fleshed-out, believable major character. I kept her in the book, but as a minor character only.

Since adopting a cat from the shelter, I've written about many feline characters.

Sulu is a remarkable cat, sweet-natured and highly intelligent. He takes a keen interest in my writing, usually snuggling on the desk between my arms as I type, watching my fingers dance across the keyboard. I've trained him to perform little circus tricks and to pose for photos. When I say 'Sulu, read' he lies down by the open book, places a paw on the page, and looks as if he's reading. When I say 'Sulu, scratch' he walks to the scratching post and scratches.

With a smart, cooperative cat like Sulu, I have a constant source of inspiration, and I can observe first-hand how a cat character would act. This is so much easier – and more believable – than my clueless attempts to write about horses.

ASSIGNMENT

Could your MC have a pet? If yes, what kind? If not, might another major characters have one? How could this animal contribute to the plot?

CHAPTER 13:
TROUBLE-SHOOTING CHARACTERS

What difficulties do you experience with your characters? Have your critique partners, beta-readers or editors told you there's a recurring problem with your characterisation?

Here are some common problems and suggested solutions.

"My characters are too alike."

This is probably because you've made them too similar to yourself. They all see the world as you do, respond to problems the way you would, make the same choices. Your characters are your creations, and subconsciously you've given them a part of your soul.

While it's good to infuse characters with something of yourself, each should have different aspect (e.g. one may have your professional ambitions, another your romantic streak, a third your fear of spiders) and none, except perhaps the MC, should match your overall personality.

To fix this problem, you need to start at the core of each character. Applying superficial fixes won't help. If you make one woman brunette and the other blonde, they'll still come across as too similar, even if you give one a passion for strawberries and a nail-biting habit while the other loves big earrings and chocolate eclairs.

Instead, look at what's deep inside them. What is this character's most deeply-held value?

Let's say one woman values honesty above all else, while for the other, diplomacy is what matters most. Given the same situation, each woman will make different choices. They will act differently, and be individuals.

By all means add some small character quirks – the oversized earrings and the addiction to chocolate eclairs – but those are just finishing touches.

"My characters are too passive."

Give them a goal, something they need to achieve. Raise the stakes, and put obstacles in their way.

You can give each character one big goal to pursue throughout the story, plus several short-term ones. Small goals can be as simple as 'to get something to eat'.

Make sure the character feels the need strongly, and give her an important or urgent reason to pursue the goal. Why does she want to get something to eat? Because she's hungry! After oversleeping, she didn't have breakfast, and then the urgent assignment at the office forced her to skip lunch. Her stomach is growling, and she fears someone will hear it, how embarrassing! Or perhaps she has a metabolic disorder and unless she eats a snack every three hours, she'll pass out. It's been three hours since she ate that apple, and she's already feeling dizzy. How can she get some food, fast?

"My characters are completely different people at the end of the novel."

Characters change – and not just the expected 'growth' over the course of the story. Often, they become different people altogether. Their values, affiliations, ambitions, fears, morals, ages, body shapes, jobs or background change, sometimes even their gender.

Every writer I know experiences this. There's only one solution: revise the book, so the character in the beginning and middle is consistent with the character at the end. Always align everything with how the character is at the end, because that's the character's 'true' identity.

If you've created a character profile at the beginning and worked from it, make sure you update it continuously. Watch out especially for any changes relating to the character's 'backstory' (what happened before the novel's events), because casual mentions of childhood experiences and teenage shenanigans can trip you up. For example, if you've changed one character's age but not another's, their shared memory of a school trip is no longer appropriate.

"My characters are not ethnically diverse."

Many readers (and most publishers) today want ethnic diversity in their books. Since this may affect acceptance by a publisher, customer reviews and sales figures, it can be a good strategy to introduce diversity as far it makes sense in the context of the story's setting.

A quick (albeit superficial) solution is to change the names of minor characters. Let's say you've written a YA (Young Adult) novel in which the MC's classmates are called John, Bill and Susan, and the teachers are Ms Jones and Dr Willborough. The publisher's editor requests that you make the book more diverse to reflect modern society. Simply change the names to Abdul, Sergej, Sunita, Ms Hernandez and Dr Wong, and you have the image of an ethnically diverse school.

For a more significant change, pick one of the major characters – perhaps the MC's sidekick – and give him a different ethnicity. Consider what it means to belong to a minority in this society – will he be barred from certain events and places, restricted in his education and career? Or does he actually get advantages as the token ethnic person in 'politically correct' contexts, or because people imagine that everyone of his race has remarkable talent?

You can write about a character who has a different heritage but has lived in this society all his life, and whose family assimilated into the local culture generations ago. This will be easiest to write.

You can also choose to write the ethnic character as someone who is outside mainstream society, perhaps from a community that preserves its own customs and traditions, or newly arrived from abroad. There will be cultural conflicts, for example, the family's expectations versus society's rules. Show how he deals with them. This requires a lot more research and cultural sensitivity to get it right without rehashing racial stereotypes. If possible, choose an ethnicity whose culture you understand or can easily research. If handled well, this will enrich your novel greatly.

"My manuscript has too many characters."

If your novel has a lot of characters, your readers may get confused, forget who is who, and struggle to understand each individual's role.

The solution: reduce the cast. Instead of two sisters, three ex-wives and four lieutenants, the MC has one of each.

Double up the function of each character. Could the MC's neighbour also be his personal trainer? Could his boss be his sister's ardent beau? Maybe the gardener doubles up as the handyman?

This not only reduces the number of characters, but it will give complexity, clarity and depth.

"Readers don't care about my characters."

Readers must care about the MC, and about most of the major characters as well.

To make a character likeable, use the techniques from Chapter 5.

Give each character a goal, something they work towards throughout the story. Readers care about characters with goals. The moment the character has a goal, readers will care for her. State her goal clearly, and remind the readers of it often.

"A minor character overshadows the major characters."

Sometimes, a minor character becomes so vivid and interesting that readers want to read about her instead of the major characters.

The solution is simple: promote her to major character. Of course, in her new role she'll have to shoulder a bigger responsibility and a heavier workload. Give her problems to solve.

Instead of creating a new role for her, you can also fire another character who isn't pulling her weight, and fill the position with the newcomer.

"A major character overshadows the MC."

Depending on the genre, certain types of major characters may be as strong and fascinating as the MC, perhaps even more so, for example, the villain in a Thriller or the love interest in a Romance.

If another major character becomes too interesting, use her as the MC in your next book! You'll enjoy writing about her, the readers will enjoy reading about her, and book sales may soar because this book promotes the next.

Have a word with the character. Ask her to hold back in this volume so she can star in the next.

"My characters all talk alike."

This is because they talk like you. You've articulated their thoughts the way you would express them.

You may have tried giving each character a typical speech quirk, and it didn't work. The result probably sounded forced.

Instead, I suggest you let people talk the way they are. Think about what kind of person the character is, where she comes from, what level of education she's had.

Pay attention to how other people in real life talk. Their speech patterns depend on their age, education level and other factors. For example, a university professor talks differently than a high-school dropout, and a teenager talks differently than her grandmother.

Personality also plays a role. For example, a self-centred person uses the words 'I, me, my, mine' in almost every sentence, while an insecure character may preface everything she says with something like "It's only my opinion..." or "I'm sorry if this isn't relevant, but..."

To learn more about this, you may want to read *Writing Vivid Dialogue,* also part of the Writer's Craft series.

"My villain is thoroughly evil, but my beta readers say he's boring."

That's because all-evil villains are boring. They're two-dimensional stereotyped characters.

To fix this, give your villain a genuine good side. Maybe he devotes himself tirelessly to caring for his ailing old parents, or he risks his life to rescue children.

My Writer's Craft guide *Writing About Villains* covers this in depth.

"My characters refuse to do what the plot requires."

The characters may simply not do what you want them to. Many authors experience this. Often, the characters say "It didn't happen that way" as if they remembered events they've already lived through.

Other characters are attention-craving divas who demand bigger roles.

With minor characters, be tough. Tell them that unless they behave, you'll write them out of the novel, replace them with someone else, or kill them off.

With major characters, it's not so easy. I've learnt to give in to their demands, because they know their story better than I do. Invariably, the story they act out is much better than what I had envisioned.

Try to negotiate a compromise. Offer them a bonus, something they really want, but they'll get it only if they do what you tell them. "If you date Mary, I'll let you drive a Rolls Royce."

When it's the main character who refuses to fall in with your plans, I recommend you go along with what she wants. This will almost certainly lead to a better plot.

However, if you need to deliver a certain type of plot with a pre-defined outcome, you can't let the characters do what they want. For example, in traditional genre Romance, the female and male leads need to enter a committed love relationship with each other, because this is the happy ending the reader has paid for. If they detest each other and refuse to pair up, you're in trouble. Your only option is to start the book afresh with new characters.

FROM MY PERSONAL EXPERIENCE

At one stage, **Dahoud,** the main character in *Storm Dancer,* insisted on getting tortured. The plot as I envisioned it didn't involve anything so gruesome, and I certainly didn't want to write a torture scene. But Dahoud insisted. I couldn't believe it. What sane person gets tortured voluntarily?

When I declined to write a torture scene into the plot, Dahoud refused to cooperate for the rest of the book. This stopped progress more effectively than any writer's block.

I gave in. I changed the plot, so Dahoud submitted himself to his vengeful enemy for torture in order to save his people. The result is moving and meaningful. Readers admire Dahoud's courage and sacrifice. Through this voluntary suffering to save others, Dahoud atones for his evil past, and redeems himself. It all made sense. When I now look at the book, I can see that the torture is an integral part of the story, and that Dahoud was right.

Merida went on strike too. I showed her smoking joy-flowers during her long captivity in the harem and becoming addicted. She demanded that I scrap those chapters and write them again, because she would never take any mind-altering substances, however dire her situation. Unless I changed that part, she would not participate in the rest of the book. I argued, I pleaded, I coaxed – in vain. Merida was such a strong-willed, principled character, there was nothing I could do but give in.

Esha was meant to be a minor character with a cameo appearance in just three scenes. But she had aspirations to be a major character, and she schemed cleverly to get a starring role. Threatening to kill her off – usually an effective approach to bring minor characters to heel – didn't help because the plot demanded her demise anyway, and she knew it.

I offered her several additional scenes, including three in her PoV. As a sweetener, I promised to give her glamorous dresses. The outfits clinched it. She agreed to go along with my plans as long as she was the best-dressed woman in every scene.

DEAR READER,

I hope you enjoyed this book and have gained many practical ideas how to bring your characters to life.

I'd love it if you could post a review on Amazon or some other book site where you have an account and posting privileges. Maybe you can mention what genre you write, and which of the techniques suggested in this guide work best for your fiction.

Email me the link to your review, and I'll send you a free review copy (ebook) of one of my other Writer's Craft books. Let me know which one you would like: *Writing Fight Scenes, Writing Scary Scenes, The Word-Loss Diet, Writing About Magic, Writing About Villains, Writing Dark Stories, Euphonics For Writers, Writing Short Stories to Promote Your Novels, Twitter for Writers, Why Does My Book Not Sell? 20 Simple Fixes, Writing Vivid Settings, How To Train Your Cat To Promote Your Book, Writing Deep Point of View, Getting Book Reviews, Writing Vivid Dialogue, Novel Revision Prompts.* You can read them in any order; just pick the one you would find most helpful right now.

My email is raynehall00000@gmail.com. Also drop me a line if you've spotted any typos which have escaped the proofreader's eagle eyes, or want to give me private feedback or have questions.

You can also contact me on Twitter: https://twitter.com/RayneHall. Tweet me that you've read this book, and I'll probably follow you back.

If you find this book helpful, it would be great if you could spread the word about it. Maybe you know other writers who would benefit.

If you want to study characterisation further, you may find *Writing Deep Point Of View* and *Writing About Villains* helpful. They can serve as a continuation to this book. I'm attaching the first chapter of *Writing Deep Point Of View.* I hope you enjoy it.

With best wishes for your writing,

Rayne Hall

ACKNOWLEDGEMENTS

Sincere thanks to the members of the Professional Authors online group who helped with advice and critiqued the individual chapters, and to the writers who beta-read the complete manuscript and gave me feedback before the final version: Ronda Del Boccio, Ede Omokhudu, Kristin Flanagan, Casey Bottono, Catherine Milos, Bill Kieffer.

The book cover design is by Erica Syverson. The book was proofread by Julia Gibbs and formatted by Bogdan Matei.

EXCERPT:
WRITING DEEP POINT OF VIEW

CHAPTER 1: FRESH PERSPECTIVES

Instead of explaining Point of View, I'll let you experience it. Let's do a quick practical exercise.

Wherever you are right now, look out of the window (or step out into the open, or do whatever comes closest). If possible, open the window and stick your head out. What do you notice?

Return to your desk or notebook, and jot down two sentences about your spontaneous observations.

You can jot down anything—the cars rushing by, the rain-heavy clouds drawing up on the horizon, the scent of lilacs, the wasps buzzing around the dumpster, the aeroplane scratching the sky, the empty beer cans in the gutter, the rain-glistening road, whatever. Don't bother writing beautiful prose—only the content matters. And only two sentences.

When you've done this—but not before—read on.

*

*

*

*

*

Have you written two sentences about what you observed outside the window? Good. Now we'll have fun.

Imagine that you're a different person. Pick one of these:

1. A 19-year-old female student, art major, currently planning to create a series of paintings of townscapes, keenly aware of colours and shapes.

2. A professional musician with sharp ears and a keen sense of rhythm.

3. An eighty-year-old man with painful arthritic knees which get worse in cold weather. He's visiting his daughter and disapproves of the place where she's living these days.

4. A retired health and safety inspector.

5. An architect whose hobby is local history.

6. A hobby gardener with a keen sense of smell.

7. A security consultant assessing the place where a foreign royal princess is going to walk among the people next week.

Once again, stick your head out of the window. What do you notice this time? Return to your desk and jot down two sentences.

I bet the observations are very different! Each time, you saw, heard and smelled the same place—but the first time you experienced it as yourself (from your Point of View) and the second time, as a fictional character (from that character's PoV).

You may want to repeat this exercise with another character from the list, to deepen your insight and practice the skill. If you're an eager learner, do all seven. This will give you a powerful understanding of how PoV works.

Now let's take it one step further: Imagine you're the main character from the story you're currently writing (or have recently finished). How would he experience this place? What would he notice above all else? Again, write two sentences.

Now you've experienced the power of PoV, this is how you will write all your fiction.

ASSIGNMENT

Repeat this exercise in a different place—perhaps when you have time to kill during a train journey or in the dentist's waiting room.

Printed in Poland
by Amazon Fulfillment
Poland Sp. z o.o., Wrocław

26818919R00047